BATS SET I

WRINKLE-FACED BATS

Tamara L. Britton
ABDO Publishing Company

visit us at
www.abdopublishing.com

Published by ABDO Publishing Company, 8000 West 78th Street, Edina, Minnesota 55439. Copyright © 2011 by Abdo Consulting Group, Inc. International copyrights reserved in all countries. No part of this book may be reproduced in any form without written permission from the publisher. The Checkerboard Library™ is a trademark and logo of ABDO Publishing Company.

Printed in the United States of America, North Mankato, Minnesota.
042010
092010

♻ PRINTED ON RECYCLED PAPER

Cover Photo: © Merlin D. Tuttle, Bat Conservation International, www.batcon.org
Interior Photos: Animals Animals p. 19; iStockphoto p. 9; © Merlin D. Tuttle, Bat
    Conservation International, www.batcon.org pp. 5, 10, 21;
    Photo Researchers pp. 11, 13; Photolibrary p. 17

Editor: BreAnn Rumsch
Art Direction & Cover Design: Neil Klinepier

Library of Congress Cataloging-in-Publication Data

Britton, Tamara L., 1963-
  Wrinkle-faced bats / Tamara L. Britton.
     p. cm. -- (Bats)
  Includes index.
  ISBN 978-1-61613-395-5
  1. Wrinkle-faced bat--Juvenile literature. I. Title.
  QL737.C57B75 2011
  599.4'5--dc22
                         2010009932

CONTENTS

WRINKLE-FACED BATS

There are more than 1,100 species of bats in the world. That's a lot of bats! Wrinkle-faced bats are a species in the family **Phyllostomidae**. As the name suggests, their little pink faces are very wrinkly!

Like all bats, wrinkle-faced bats are mammals. One-quarter of all mammals are bats. Like other mammals, bats have hair. And, mother bats give birth to live babies and feed them with milk. Yet bats can do something no other mammal can do. They can fly!

Some people are afraid of bats. Yet, bats are helpful. Each year, insect-eating bats eat millions of insect pests. Bats that eat fruits and flowers help plants reproduce. These beneficial creatures are an important part of their ecosystem.

Wrinkle-faced bats are sometimes called old man bats!

Where They're Found

Bats can be found all over the world except the polar regions and a few ocean islands. They live on every continent except Antarctica. Wrinkle-faced bats live in North, Central, and South America.

In North America, the wrinkle-faced bat's range begins in northern Mexico. It reaches from the state of Sinaloa east to the state of Tamaulipas. From there, the bats live throughout Central America. Their range extends south to Venezuela in South America. They also live on the island of Trinidad.

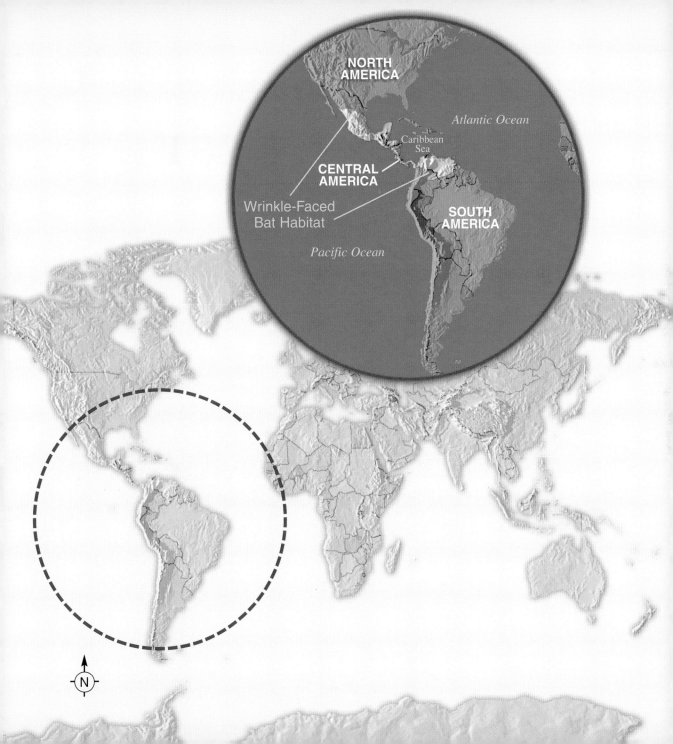

NORTH
AMERICA

Atlantic Ocean

Caribbean
Sea

CENTRAL
AMERICA

Wrinkle-Faced
Bat Habitat

SOUTH
AMERICA

Pacific Ocean

N

WHERE THEY LIVE

With such a wide range, wrinkle-faced bats have many **habitats**. They live in both moist and dry climates. They live in **deciduous** and evergreen forests.

Wrinkle-faced bats prefer to **roost** in thick **foliage**. The bats roost under the leaves of trees. Usually, there are about 12 bats roosting in each tree. Sometimes, a single bat roosts in a tree by itself. Or, two bats may roost together. Males and females share the same roost but hang out apart from one another.

To roost, bats hang upside down by their feet. Their feet have five toes. Each toe has a sharp, curved claw. To **roost**, wrinkle-faced bats grab onto a surface with their claws. When they relax, a **tendon** in each foot closes their claws on the roosting site.

Wrinkle-faced bats like to roost in papaya trees.

SIZES

Wrinkle-faced bats are not big bats. They grow 2 to 3 inches (5 to 7.5 cm) long. Their **wingspan** measures about 9 inches (23 cm). They weigh just 0.5 to 1 ounce (17 to 28 g).

Some bats are much smaller than wrinkle-faced bats. Kitti's hog-nosed bats grow to only 1 inch

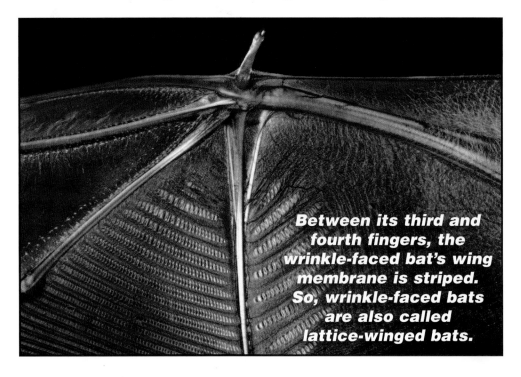

Between its third and fourth fingers, the wrinkle-faced bat's wing membrane is striped. So, wrinkle-faced bats are also called lattice-winged bats.

(2.5 cm) long. Their **wingspan** is 6 inches (15 cm). These bats are so tiny they are called bumblebee bats!

In comparison, flying fox bats are much larger. The largest can grow more than 16 inches (40 cm) long. Its wingspan reaches more than 5 feet (1.5 m)!

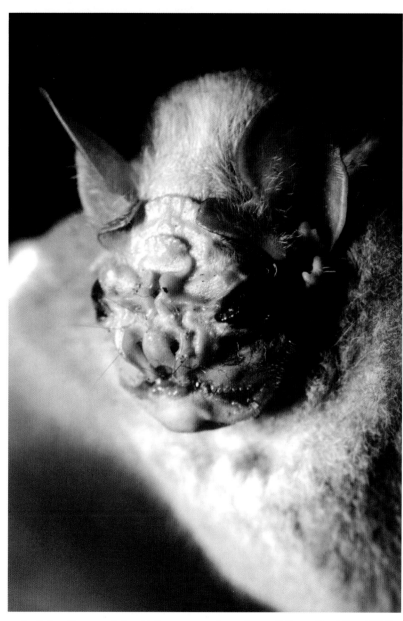

The wrinkle-faced bat has a short, wide skull. This gives it the strongest bite of any bat of its size!

SHAPES

Wrinkle-faced bats are unusual looking! Their short, wide faces are hairless. Pink, fleshy folds of skin surround the nose and mouth.

A male wrinkle-faced bat has a fold of skin under its chin. When **roosting**, the male will pull it up over his face. The skin fold has transparent spots where it covers the eyes. Scientists believe these spots allow the bat to see through the skin.

Though their faces have no fur, wrinkle-faced bats do have short, silky fur on their bodies. It ranges from yellow brown to dark brown. The fur on the bat's underside is lighter than the fur on its back. Each shoulder has a small spot of white fur.

Wrinkle-faced bats have two arms. Each arm has a hand with four fingers and a thumb. The thumb has a claw that helps the bat grip surfaces.

The wings are thin, elastic **membranes**. They stretch between the bat's fingers, body, and legs. Between the bat's second and third fingers, the membrane is transparent.

Most bats have short tails. A few have long tails. But wrinkle-faced bats have no tail at all!

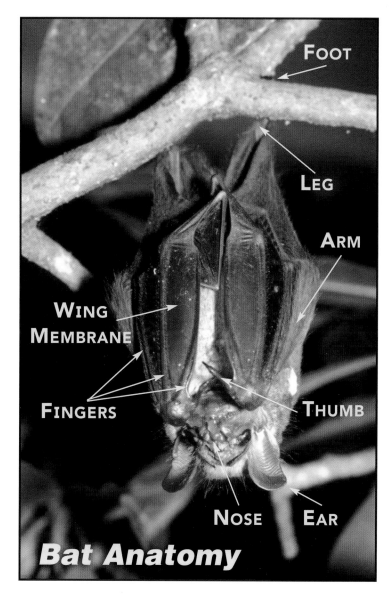

FOOT

LEG

ARM

WING MEMBRANE

FINGERS

THUMB

NOSE

EAR

Bat Anatomy

SENSES

Wrinkle-faced bats have the same five senses as humans. In addition, these **nocturnal** creatures use echolocation to move around in the dark.

To echolocate, a bat makes high-pitched sounds from its throat or nose. These sounds go out and bounce off objects such as trees, buildings, or insects.

The sounds return to the bat as echoes. The echoes tell the bat the size and location of objects. Bats use this information to fly safely, find food, and avoid danger.

Sound wave sent out by bat

Echo wave received by bat

DEFENSE

Many predators think wrinkle-faced bats make a good meal. Cats, dogs, raccoons, and skunks eat bats. Owls, hawks, falcons, snakes, and large frogs snack on them, too. Large spiders devour bats that get caught in their webs. Even worse, some bats eat other bats!

Since most bats are **nocturnal**, they are out and about at night. This helps them avoid the predators that are out hunting during the day.

For additional protection, bats look for safe, secure places in which to **roost**. Even if a predator finds a wrinkle-faced bat's roost, the bat may still be safe. The bat's brown fur makes it hard for predators to see it in its **habitat**.

Bats can change their flight path to avoid predators. However, they are not always successful.

FOOD

Little is known of the wrinkle-faced bat's feeding habits. However, scientists have determined that the bats eat fruit. Wrinkle-faced bats like the soft, mushy parts of fruits such as bananas, papayas, and mangoes.

To eat, wrinkle-faced bats suck the fruit into their mouths. Many small bumps line the skin between their lips and gums. The bats strain the fruit **pulp** through these bumps as they eat.

What are the wrinkly skin folds on the bat's face for? Some scientists believe they direct fruit juices into the bat's mouth as it eats.

18

BABIES

Most bats have just one baby each year. Some species can have one baby in the spring and another during the rainy season. Wrinkle-faced bats reproduce once or twice a year. The female has one baby each time. The baby bat is called a pup.

A pup is very big at birth. A newborn bat often weighs 25 percent of its mother's weight! After it is born, the pup climbs up onto its mother's chest to nurse.

The mother bat needs a lot of energy to care for her pup. She must hold a big baby and produce enough milk to keep it fed. So while nursing, the mother bat must find more food than usual.

At first, the mother bat takes her baby along when she gathers food. When the pup is older, it stays behind at the **roost**. Upon returning, the mother bat can find her pup by its special smell and sounds.

Scientists still have much to discover about the wrinkle-faced bat. As they continue their work, we will learn more about these fascinating creatures!

Only male wrinkle-faced bats have the skin fold under the chin. So, scientists believe it may be important for reproduction.

GLOSSARY

deciduous (dih-SIH-juh-wuhs) - shedding leaves each year. Deciduous forests have trees or shrubs that do this.

foliage - the leaves of one or more plants, especially growing leaves.

habitat - a place where a living thing is naturally found.

membrane - a thin, easily bent layer of animal tissue.

nocturnal - active at night.

Phyllostomidae (fihl-uh-STOH-mih-dee) - the scientific name for a family of New World leaf-nosed bats.

pulp - the soft, juicy part of a fruit.

roost - to perch or settle down to rest. A roost is a place, such as a cave or a tree, where animals rest.

tendon - a band of tough fibers that joins a muscle to another body part, such as a bone.

wingspan - the distance from one wing tip to the other when the wings are spread.

WEB SITES

To learn more about wrinkle-faced bats, visit ABDO Publishing Company on the World Wide Web at **www.abdopublishing.com**. Web sites about wrinkle-faced bats are featured on our Book Links page. These links are routinely monitored and updated to provide the most current information available.

INDEX